The Workers' Library. First Series

WILL THE BOLSHEVIKS MAINTAIN POWER?

Will the Bolsheviks Maintain Power?

BY
N. LENIN

SUTTON PUBLISHING

The Labour Publishing Company edition
first published in 1922

First published in this edition by
Sutton Publishing Limited
Phoenix Mill · Thrupp · Stroud
Gloucestershire · GL5 2BU

ISBN 0-7509-1677-X

Produced by offset from the
Labour Publishing Company edition of 1922.
Printed in Great Britain by
WBC Limited, Bridgend.

WILL THE BOLSHEVIKS MAINTAIN POWER?

I

WHAT is it on which all lines of thought are agreed, all—from the *Retch* to the *Novaya Zhizhn* inclusive —from the Cadet-Kornilovists to the semi-Bolsheviks—all, in fact, with the exception of the Bolsheviks?

It is in the conviction that the Bolsheviks will never make up their minds to take the whole governmental power into their own hands alone, or, should they dare do so and assume power, that they will be incapable of retaining it for any length of time.

Should anyone remark that the question of the complete assumption of power by the Bolsheviks alone is a question of no political reality, that only some "fanatic" imbued with colossal conceit could consider it for

Will the Bolsheviks

a moment to have any reality, we can refute him by quoting the exact declarations of the most responsible and most influential political parties and tendencies of various "shades."

But first a word or two regarding the first question : will the Bolsheviks decide to take complete power into their own hands? I have already had occasion to reply to this question with a categorical affirmative at the All-Russian Soviet Congress, in a remark I was compelled to shout out during one of Tseretelli's ministerial speeches. And I have met no declaration by the Bolsheviks either in the Press or verbal that we must not assume power alone. I still maintain the view that a political party in general, and the party of the premier class in particular, would have no right to existence, would be unworthy of considering itself a party, would be a pitiable cipher in every sense, were it to refuse to seize power when an opportunity occurs for it to do so.

Maintain Power?

Let us now quote the declarations of the Cadets, the Socialist-Revolutionaries and the semi-Bolsheviks (I would rather say quarter-Bolsheviks), regarding the question under discussion.

Leading article from the *Retch*, September 16th:—

"In the Alexandra Theatre there was complete discordance and confusion, and the Socialist press reflects the same picture. Only the views of the Bolsheviks are characterised by their definiteness and directness. At the convention these are the views of the minority; in the Soviets their influence is always increasing. But in spite of all their wordy passion, their arrogant phrases, their demonstrations of self-confidence, the Bolsheviks, with the exception of a few fanatics, are only brave in words. They would not attempt to take "complete power" on their own initiative. Disorganisers and disrupters *par excellence*, they are in essence cowards, understanding quite well in their heart of hearts both their personal ignorance and the ephemeral nature of their present successes. They know, just as well as we all do, that the first day of their final victory would also be the first day of their headlong fall.

"Irresponsible in their very nature, anarchists in principle and practice, they cannot be considered as anything more than a particular variety of political thought, or more correctly as one of its aberrations. The best means of getting rid of Bolshevism for a long period of years, or of destroying it, would be to entrust its leaders with the fate of the country. And were it not for the consciousness of the inadmissible and disastrous nature of the plans they would adopt one might, in despair, decide even on such a heroic step. Happily, we repeat, these dismal heroes of the day do not themselves really aim at the seizure of complete power. Under no conditions could they become capable of constructive work,

Maintain Power ?

Thus all their definiteness and directness are limited to the sphere of the
political platform and to fine literary
efforts at meetings. In actual practice
their position cannot be taken into account from any point of view. However, in one connection it has a certain
practical result. It unites all other
shades of 'Socialist thought' in a
common antagonism to it."

Thus reason the Cadets. And now,
here is the point of view of the largest
"predominant and governing" party in
Russia, the Socialist-Revolutionaries,
also in an unsigned, and therefore
editorial, leader of their official organ,
Dielo Naroda, September 21st :—

"Should the bourgeoisie be unwilling
to work together with the democracy
up to the calling of the Constituent
Assembly on the basis of the platform
laid down by the convention, then
*the Coalition must arise from within the
constitution of the assembly.*

"This is a heavy sacrifice on the part

of the defenders of the Coalition, *but the propagandists of the idea of a 'straight line' power must make up their minds to it too.* But we are afraid there may be no agreement as to this. Then there remains a third and last combination. It will be the *duty* of that section of the convention to organise the government which *on principle* defended the idea of its homogeneity.

"Let us say it quite definitely—*the Bolsheviks will be obliged to form the cabinet.* Working with the greatest energy, they filled the revolutionary democracy with hatred of the Coalition, promising it every blessing once they had got rid of the policy of 'understandings,' and throwing on the shoulders of such 'understandings' all the misfortunes of the country.

"If they have really kept account of their *agitation,* if they have *not deceived the masses, they are in duty bound* to pay the bills of exchange they handed out right and left.

"The question is quite clear; they

must not be allowed to make useless efforts to hide behind hastily concocted theories of the impossibility of their taking power.

"The democracy will accept no such theories.

"At the same time the supporters of the Coalition must guarantee them full support. These are the three combinations, the three ways that stand before us—there are no others." (The italics are those of the *Dielo Naroda* itself.)

Thus the S.R.'s. Here finally is the position—if the attempt to sit between two stools can be called a position— of the "Novaya Zhizhnist" quarter-Bolsheviks, taken from the editorial leader of the *Novaya Zhizhn*, September 23rd :—

"If the Coalition with Konovalov and Kishkin is again formed, then it will mean nothing else than a new capitulation of the democracy and the rejection of the resolution of the convention regarding a responsible government favourable to the platform of August 14th. . . .

"A homogeneous ministry of Mensheviks and S.R.'s will as little be able to feel its responsibility as did the responsible Socialist ministers in the Coalition Cabinet. . . . Such a government would not only be incapable of attracting to itself the live forces of the Revolution, but it could not even count on any active support from the vanguard of the proletariat.

"Nevertheless, it would not be a better, but a much worse way out of the position—in fact not a way out at all, but simply a catastrophe—to form another type of homogeneous cabinet —a government of the proletariat and the poorest peasantry. Such a demand, it is true, is not formulated by anyone except in certain occasional, timid, and subsequently systematically 'explained' remarks of the *Rabotchi Put*." (This glaring untruth is written "bravely" by responsible publicists, forgetting even the leader of the *Dielo Naroda* of September 21st.)

"The Bolsheviks have unofficially revived the demand for all power to the Soviets. This demand was dropped when, after the July days, the Soviets, in the form of the Central Executive Committee, definitely took up an active anti-Bolshevik attitude. Now, however, the 'Soviet line' can not only be considered to have become straightened out, but there is every reason for thinking that the proposed congress of Soviets will give a Bolshevik majority. Under such conditions the resurrection by the Bolsheviks of the cry 'All power to the Soviets' is a tactical step directed straight towards the dictatorship of the proletariat and the 'poorest peasantry.' True, by Soviets are also meant the Soviets of peasant deputies, and thus the Bolshevik demand presupposes a power resting on the overwhelming majority of the whole democracy of Russia. But in this case the cry 'All power to the

Will the Bolsheviks

Soviets,' is deprived of all independent meaning, since the Soviets are thus made almost identical in their composition with the preliminary parliament formed by the convention. . . ." (This statement of the *Novaya Zhizhn* is the most shameless lie, and amounts to the declaration that the apology for a counterfeit democracy is almost identical with democracy. The preliminary parliament is only a fraud pretending that the will of the minority of the people—particularly that of the Kaskovs, Berkenheims, Tchaikovskys and Company — is the will of the majority. That, in the first place. Secondly, even the peasant Soviets faked by the Avxsentievs and Tchaikovskys yielded such a high percentage of opponents to the Coalition in the convention, that together with the Soviets of workers' and soldiers' deputies there would have been an *absolute overthrow of the Coalition*. And thirdly, "Power to the Soviets" means that the power of the peasant Soviets would have been largely spread over the villages, and in these a majority of the poorest peasantry is assured.)

"If it is one and the same thing, then the Bolshevik demand must be removed from the order of the day without delay. If, however, 'Power to the Soviets' only conceals dictatorship of the proletariat, then such a power would but signify the disaster and wreck of the revolution.

"Is it necessary to prove that the proletariat, isolated not only from the other classes of the country but from the really living forces of the democracy, will be unable technically to control the government apparatus and to set it into motion under the present exceptionally difficult conditions; further, that the proletariat will be incapable of resisting all the pressure of the antagonistic forces, which will sweep away not only the dictatorship of the proletariat but in addition also the whole revolution?

"The only power which would correspond to the demands of the moment

The Bolsheviks

is a coalition within the democracy, a coalition which would really be only partial."

We apologise to the reader for the long quotations, but they were absolutely essential. It was necessary to present an exact view of the position of the various parties opposing the Bolsheviks. It was necessary to show in detail the highly important fact that all these parties have recognised the question of the seizure of complete power by the Bolsheviks alone not only as a very practical question but as an actual question of the day.

II

LET us pass now to the analysis of the reasons on the strength of which "all," from the Cadets to the Novaya Zhizhnists, are convinced that the Bolsheviks will be unable to retain power.

The sedate *Retch* brings forward practically no argument whatever. It merely pours out on the Bolsheviks streams of the most choice and human invective.

The quotations cited by us show, amongst other things, how very wrong it would be to think that the *Retch* is cunningly provoking the Bolsheviks into seizing power and that therefore we should be careful, since what the enemy advises must certainly be dangerous! If, instead of properly considering general concrete facts, we allow ourselves to be persuaded that the bourgeoisie is "provoking" us to take power, we shall find that we have been made fools of by the bourgeoisie. For, undoubtedly, it will always prophesy a million misfortunes from the assumption of power by the Bolsheviks. It will always cry in a fury: "Better get rid of the Bolsheviks all at once for 'many years' by letting them attain power and then striking them over the head." Such cries are also "provocation" if you like, only, on the other hand, the Cadets and the bourgeoisie do not "advise" and have never "advised" us to seize power; they only endeavour to frighten us by the so-called insoluble problems of power. No, we must not allow ourselves to be disconcerted by the shouts of the scared bourgeoisie. We must remember well that we have never placed before ourselves "insoluble" social problems, but that the *quite* soluble problems of immediate steps towards Socialism, as the only way out of an extremely difficult position, will only be solved by the dictatorship of the proletariat and of the poorest peasantry. Victory, and solid victory, is now more than ever, more than anywhere, assured to the proletariat in Russia if it seizes power.

Let us discuss in purely business fashion the concrete conditions which may render unfavourable this or that particular moment, but let us not allow ourselves to be frightened for one moment by the wild volleys of the bourgeoisie, and let us not forget that the question of the seizure of power by the Bolsheviks is becoming essentially a question of the day. An immeasurably great danger is now threatening our party if we forget this, or should we concede that the seizure of power is premature. In this connection there can now be no question of "prematurity." Of a million chances all except perhaps one or two are in its favour.

Regarding the infuriated abuse of the *Retch*, it can and must be repeated:

Will the Bolsheviks

We hear sounds of approbation—not in the dulcet sounds of praise, but in the wild shouts of irritation! The fact that the bourgeoisie hates us so madly is one of the most evident proofs of the truth that we are correctly indicating to the people the ways and means for the overthrow of the supremacy of the bourgeoisie.

Dielo Naroda, this once and as a rare exception, did not think fit to honour us with its abuse, but it has not brought forward any shadow of proof. Only in an indirect way, in the form of a hint, it seeks to frighten us by the prospect. "The Bolsheviks will be obliged to form a Cabinet." We admit fully that in trying to frighten us the S.R.'s are themselves most sincerely scared—scared to death by the phantom of the terrorised Liberals. Similarly I admit that S.R.'s in some specially high-placed and specially rotten institutions like the Central Executive Committee and such-like "contact" committees ("contiguous" with the Cadets, or, more

simply, boon friends of the Cadets),
are successful in frightening some one
or other of the Bolsheviks; for, in
the first place, the atmosphere in all
these Central Executive Committees,
in the preliminary parliament, and
so forth, is abominable, poisonous and
debilitating, and to breathe it for any
length of time is bad for anyone; and
secondly, sincerity is contagious, and
the sincerely frightened philistine is
capable of transforming temporarily
here and there even a revolutionary
into a philistine.

But however comprehensible from
the "human" point of view is this
sincere terror of the S.R. who has the
misfortune to be a minister with the
Cadets, or who is in a ministering position before the Cadets, yet to allow
oneself to be frightened means to make
a political mistake which may only too
readily become something bordering on
the betrayal of the proletariat. Such
are your skilful arguments, gentlemen.
You need not hope that we shall allow

ourselves to be frightened by your own terror.

Arguments to the point we find this time only in the *Novaya Zhizhn*. This time the journal comes out in a rôle that suits it much better, the rôle of an advocate of the bourgeoisie, rather than in one that quite evidently shocks this thoroughly pleasant lady, that of defender of the Bolsheviks. The advocate has advanced six arguments:

1. The proletariat is "isolated from the other classes of the country."
2. It is "isolated from the real living forces of the democracy."
3. It "will be unable to control the technical State machine."
4. It "will be unable to set this machine in motion."
5. "The position is exceptionally complicated."
6. It "will be incapable of withstanding the whole pressure of antagonistic forces which will sweep away not only the dictatorship of the

proletariat but in addition the
whole revolution."

The first argument is stated by the
Novaya Zhizhn so clumsily as to be
positively ridiculous, for we know but
three classes in the capitalist and semi-
capitalist society, the bourgeoisie, the
small bourgeoisie (with the peasantry
as its chief representative) and the proletariat. What sense then is there in
talking about the isolation of the proletariat from the other classes, seeing
that it is a question of the struggle of the
proletariat against the bourgeoisie, of
the revolution against the bourgeoisie?
Probably the *Novaya Zhizhn* meant
to say that the proletariat is isolated
from the peasantry, for surely there
could be no question here of the landowners. But they could not say directly
and clearly that the proletariat is now
isolated from the peasantry, for the
glaring untruth of such a statement
would be too strikingly self-evident. It
is difficult to imagine that in a capitalist

country the proletariat should be so little isolated from the middle class, and, note, in a revolution *against the bourgeoisie,* as is the proletariat now in Russia.

We have as objective and indisputable facts the most recent figures in the voting for and against coalition with the bourgeoisie in the " special classes " of the Tseretelli " Bulygin Duma,"—that is, the notorious " Democratic " convention. Let us take the class of Soviets; we find:—

	For Coalition	Against Coalition
Soviets of Workers' and Soldiers' Deputies	83	192
Soviets of Peasants' Deputies	102	70
All the Soviets	185	262

Thus the majority as a whole is on the side of the proletarian demand—*against* Coalition with the bourgeoisie. And we have seen above that even the Cadets are forced to admit the growing influence of the Bolsheviks in the

Maintain Power?

Soviets. But we have here a convention summoned by the Soviet leaders of *yesterday*, and by the S.R.'s and Mensheviks who have an assured majority in the central institutions. It is clear that the real predominance of the Bolsheviks in the Soviets is here *minimised*.

Both on the question of coalition with the bourgeoisie and on the immediate handing over of the landed estates to the peasant committees, the Bolsheviks already have a *majority* in the Soviets of workers', soldiers' and peasants' deputies—the *majority of the nation*, the majority of the small bourgeoisie. The *Rabotchi Put*, No. 19, September 24th, cites from No. 25 of the S.R. organ, *Znamia Truda*, an account of a convention of local Soviets of peasant deputies held in Petrograd on September 18th. At this convention the Executive Committees of four peasant Soviets (Kostroma, Moscow, Samara and Tver districts) expressed themselves in favour of unlimited coalition.

Will the Bolsheviks

For coalition without the Cadets there were the Executive Committees of three districts and two armies (Vladimir, Ryazan and the Black Sea provinces). Against coalition there were the Executive Committees of *twenty-three* districts and *four* armies.

Thus, *the majority of the peasantry are against the Coalition!*

Here, Messieurs, is your "isolation of the proletariat."

We must note by the way that *for* coalition there were three border districts, Samara, Tver and Black Sea, where there is a comparatively large number of rich peasants, big landowners, working their land with hired labour, and also four industrial districts (Vladimir, Ryazan, Kostroma and Moscow) where also the peasant bourgeoisie is more numerous than in the majority of the Russian districts. It would be interesting to gather more detailed facts on this subject and to ascertain whether any information is available regarding the *poorest* peasantry in the districts containing a preponderance of "rich" peasants.

Further, it is interesting to note that the "national groups" yielded a considerable majority to the opponents of Coalition—namely, 40 votes against 15. The harsh, violent, annexationist policy of the Bonapartist Kerensky and Company towards the dependent nationalities of Russia has borne fruit. The wide masses of the population of the oppressed nations—that is, the masses of the small bourgeoisie amongst them—trust the Russian proletariat more than they do the bourgeoisie, for history has here brought upon the order of the day the struggle for freedom of the oppressed nations against their oppressors. The bourgeoisie has easily betrayed the cause of the liberation of the oppressed nations, the proletariat is true to the cause of freedom.

The national and agrarian questions —these are root questions for the petty bourgeois masses of the population of Russia at the present time. This is indisputable. On both questions the proletariat is, to a remarkable extent, secured from isolation. The proletariat has behind it the majority of the nation. On both questions it and *it only* is capable of pursuing such a decided, truly " revolutionary - democratic " policy, as can assure immediately to a proletarian government not only the support of the majority of the population, but a veritable explosion of revolutionary enthusiasm amongst the masses; since for the first time the masses would be met by the government, not with a merciless oppression of the peasantry by the landowners, of the Ukrainians by the Great Russians, as under Tsarism: not with attempts to follow the same policy under a Republic, only camouflaged by a few high-sounding phrases: not with cavilling, insults, chicanery, dilatoriness, hauteur, evasions (with all of which Kerensky rewards the peasantry and the oppressed nationalities); but with warm sympathy expressed by deeds:

Maintain Power?

immediate and revolutionary measures against the landowners, the immediate grant of full freedom for Finland, Ukraine, White Russia, the Mussulmans, and so forth.

The S.R.'s and Mensheviks know all this very well, and for this reason they drag the half-Cadet chiefs of the Co-operators to assist in their reactionary democratic policy *against* the masses. Because of all this, they will never dare to consult the masses, to institute a referendum or even a vote in all the local Soviets, in all local organisations, on definite points of practical policy, for instance, on the questions whether all the land of the big estates should be given immediately to the peasant committees, whether the particular demands of the Finns and Ukrainians should be conceded, and so forth.

And what about the question of peace, that cardinal question of the whole of modern life? The proletariat is isolated from the other classes. . . . The proletariat here comes forward in truth

The Bolsheviks

as the representative of the *whole* nation, of all that is vital and honest in *all* classes, of the vast majority of the middle class; for only the proletariat, having attained power, will immediately propose a just peace to all the fighting nations. Only the proletariat will go the length of really *revolutionary* measures (the publication of secret treaties, etc.) so as to obtain at the earliest moment as just a peace as possible. No, the gentlemen of the *Novaya Zhizhn*, screaming so lustily about the isolation of the proletariat, only express thereby their own subjective terror induced by the bourgeoisie. The objective position of affairs in Russia is undoubtedly such that *just at the present time* the proletariat is not "isolated" from the majority of the small bourgeoisie. Just now, indeed, after the pitiful attempts of the " Coalition," the proletariat has on its side the sympathy of the *majority* of the nation. *This* ground for the retention of power by the Bolsheviks is quite self-evident.

III

THE second argument consists in
the assumption that the proletariat is "isolated from the really living
forces of the democracy." What this
means it is impossible to understand.
It is probably Greek, as the French say
in such a case.

The writers of the *Novaya Zhizhn* are
of the ministerial kind. They would
have been quite suitable as ministers
under the Cadets, for from such
ministers one demands exactly this
ability to utter fine-sounding, flattering
phrases in which there is no sense
whatever, whereby one can conceal
any and every rottenness, and which
are therefore assured of the applause
of the Imperialists and of the Imperialist Socialists. The applause of
the Cadets, of Breshkovskaia, and of
Plekhanov and Company is guaranteed

the "Novaya Zhizhnists" by their statement that the proletariat is isolated from the really vital forces of the democracy; for in an *indirect* way it means, or will be understood as though it meant, that the Cadets, Breshkovskaia, Plekhanov, Kerensky and Company "are the living forces of the democracy."

This is untrue. These are but shrivelled forces. This has been proved by the history of the Coalition. Cowed by the bourgeoisie and the bourgeois-intellectual environment, the "Novaya Zhizhnists" recognise as "living" the *right* wing of the S.R. and Menshevik groups, such as the "Volia Naroda," "Yedinstvo," and so forth, which differ vitally from the Cadets in nothing. We, on the other hand, recognise as "living" only what is bound up with the masses, not with the kulaks (profiteers), only that which has been led by experience of the Coalition to turn away from it. "The active living forces" of the small bourgeois democracy are represented by the left wings of the S.R.'s and the Mensheviks. The strengthening of this left wing, particularly after the July counter-revolution, is one of the most certain signs that the proletariat is not isolated.

This has become still more evident just lately by the wavering towards the left of the S.R. Centre, proved by Tchernoff's declaration of September 24th, that his group cannot support the new Coalition with Kishkin and Company. This inclination towards the left of the S.R. Centre, which until now has formed an overwhelming majority of the representatives of the S.R. party—the party which, as a result of the number of votes obtained by it in the towns and particularly in the villages, occupies a supreme and dominating position—proves that the statement quoted by us from the *Dielo Naroda* regarding the necessity for the democracy, under certain circumstances, to "guarantee full support" to a purely Bolshevik government, is, at any rate, not a mere phrase.

Such facts as the refusal of the S.R. Centre to support a Coalition with Kishkin, and the predominance of the *opponents* of Coalition among the Menshevik - patriots in the provinces (Jordania in the Caucasus, and so on), form an objective proof that a certain section of the masses following, until now, the Mensheviks and S.R.'s will *support* a purely Bolshevik government.

It is just from the *living* forces of the democracy that the Russian proletariat is *not* now isolated.

IV

ARGUMENT the third: "The proletariat will be unable to control the technical apparatus of government." This, we grant, is the most usual, the most plausible argument. It deserves most careful attention both for this reason and because it really indicates one of the most *serious*, one of the most *difficult* problems confronting the victorious proletariat. There is no doubt these problems are very difficult, but if, whilst calling ourselves Socialists, we point out this difficulty only for the purpose of *avoiding* the solution of these problems, then, in practice there will be no difference between us and the servants of the bourgeoisie. The difficulties of the problems arising from the proletarian revolution should only lead the supporters of the proletariat to a closer and more concrete study of

Will the Bolsheviks

the methods whereby to solve these problems.

By the apparatus of government is meant, first of all, the standing army, police and officialdom. In speaking of the proletariat being unable to control this apparatus, the writers of the *Novaya Zhizhn* reveal the greatest ignorance and disinclination to take into account either the facts of life or the views expressed long ago in Bolshevik literature.

The writers of the *Novaya Zhizhn* all consider themselves, if not Marxists, at any rate as being acquainted with Marxism and as educated Socialists. And Marx has taught us, from the experience of the attempts of the Paris Commune, that the proletariat *cannot* simply take possession of the ready-made State machine and set it in motion for its own purposes, that the proletariat must *break up* this machine and replace it by a new one. (This is treated in detail in the author's pamphlet, *The State and Revolution* —

Maintain Power ?

the Teaching of Marx on the State and the Problems confronting the Proletariat in the Revolution.) This new State machine was created by the Paris Commune, and of the same type of State machine are the Russian Soviets of workers', soldiers' and peasants' deputies. I have pointed this out many times, beginning August 4th, 1917. This is mentioned in the resolutions of Bolshevik Conferences and in Bolshevik literature. The *Novaya Zhizhn* could of course announce its complete disagreement both with Marx and with the Bolsheviks, but for a journal that has so often loftily abused the Bolsheviks for their "frivolous" attitude towards difficult questions, simply to evade this subject signifies the issue of a certificate of their own intellectual poverty.

The proletariat *cannot* "take possession of the State machine and set it into motion," but it can *destroy* all that is oppressive, merely routine, incurably bourgeois in the old State machine and put in its place its own new apparatus. This machine is exactly the Soviets of workers', soldiers' and peasants' deputies.

One cannot but regard it as marvellous that the *Novaya Zhizhn* has quite forgotten about this "State apparatus." In conducting thus their theoretical discussions, the writers of the *Novaya Zhizhn* really do in the sphere of political theory exactly what the Cadets are doing in the sphere of political practice. For if the proletariat really need no new State apparatus, then the Soviets lose their right to existence. In that case the Cadet-Kornilovists are quite right in their efforts to nullify the Soviets. This marvellous theoretical mistake and political blindness of the *Novaya Zhizhn* is so much the more amazing in that even the Menshevik Internationalists (with whom the *Novaya Zhizhn* went in a block at the last municipal elections at Petrograd) have shown in this question a certain approach towards

Maintain Power ?

the Bolsheviks. Thus we read in the declaration of the Soviet majority read by Com. Martov at the Democratic Convention: ". . . The Soviets of deputies of workers, soldiers and peasants, created in the first days by the mighty impulse of the real national creative genius, formed that new tissue of the revolutionary State which has replaced the decayed State tissue of the old regime. . . ." This is expressed a trifle too prettily—that is, the pretentiousness of the language here conceals the insufficient clarity of political meaning. The Soviets have *not yet* replaced the old "tissue," and this old tissue is not the State of the old regime, but the State of both Tsarism and the bourgeois Republic. Still Martov here stands two heads above the men of the *Novaya Zhizhn.*

The Soviets are the new State machinery. In the first place, they give expression to the armed force of the workers and peasants, in such a way, however, that this force is not

Will the Bolsheviks

divorced from the people, as was the force of the old standing army, but is bound up with them as closely as possible. In a military sense this force is incomparably greater than the former; in relation to the revolution it is second to none. Secondly, the link of this machinery with the masses, with the majority of the people, is so intimate, so indissoluble, so readily verified and renewable, that nothing like it is even approached in the former State. Thirdly, this machinery, because it is elective and its constitution is revocable in accordance with the will of the people without any bureaucratic formalities, is far more democratic than that of the old governments. Fourthly, it yields a firm connection with the most various industries and professions, thus facilitating all sorts of most radical reforms without any bureaucracy. Fifthly, it gives form to the organisation of the vanguard, that is to the most conscious, most energetic, most progressive section of the *oppressed* classes of the workers and peasants, and is thus an apparatus whereby the vanguard of the oppressed classes can uplift, educate and lead in its train the *whole gigantic mass* of these classes which until now have stood quite outside all political life, outside history. Sixthly, it makes it possible to unite the advantages of parliamentarism with the advantages of immediate and direct democracy —that is, to unite in the persons of elected representatives of the people both legislative and *executive* functions. In comparison with bourgeois parliamentarism it is a step forward in the development of democracy which has a historical world significance.

Our Soviets of 1905 were only, so to speak, an embryo in the womb, for they only existed for a few weeks. It is quite clear that in the circumstances of the time there could be no question of their all-round development. And in the 1917 revolution there can as yet be no question of it, for a period of a few months is too little, and, above all, the S.R. and Menshevik leaders of the Soviets have *prostituted* them, have degraded them to the rôle of mere talking shops, and of accessories to the Coalition policy. The Soviets were rotting and decaying rapidly under the leadership of the Liebers, Dans, Tseretellis, and Tchernovs. The Soviets can only develop properly and expand to the full their promise and capabilities when they assume *full* powers of government, for otherwise they have *nothing* to do; they then become simply embryos (and one cannot remain an embryo too long) or mere playthings. "Divided power" signifies the paralysis of the Soviets.

Had not the popular creative genius of the revolutionary classes given rise to the Soviets, the proletarian revolution in Russia would have been hopeless, for there is no doubt that with the old State machine the proletariat could not have retained power, and to create a new power all of a sudden is impossible.

Maintain Power ?

The miserable history of the prostitution of the Soviets by Tseretelli and Tchernov, the history of the "Coalition," is, at the same time, the history of the freeing of the Soviets from petty bourgeois illusions, of their passing through a "cleansing station," of their practical study of all the abominations and filth of *all and every* bourgeois Coalition. Let us hope that this "cleansing process" has not undermined the Soviets, but has only tempered them.

The most difficult problem of a proletarian revolution is the realisation on a national scale of a very exact and honest accounting and control, the control by the *workers* of production and distribution of the products. When the writers of the *Novaya Zhizhn* reproached us with falling into syndicalism when we put forward the demand of "workers control," this reproach was merely a specimen of a silly schoolboy application of "Marxism," which, instead of having been thought out, has been only learned by rote after the manner of Struve.

Will the Bolsheviks

Syndicalism either rejects the revolutionary dictatorship of the proletariat, or shifts it, like political power in general, to the ninth place. We give it first place. If we talk simply in the spirit of the "Novaya Zhizhnists"—not workers' control but State control—then we merely get a bourgeois reformist phrase, in fact a pure Cadet formula, for the Cadets have nothing against the *participation* of the workers in "State" control. The Cadet-Kornilovists know very well that such participation is the best way for the bourgeoisie to deceive the workers, the best method of subtle political bribery known to the Guchkovs, Nikitins, Prokopovitchs, Tseretellis, and all of that kidney.

When we speak of "workers' control," placing this cry side by side with the dictatorship of the proletariat and always as resulting therefrom, we make clear thereby what State we have in mind. The State is an organ for the supremacy of a class. Which? If the bourgeoisie, then this is just the Cadet-

Maintain Power ?

Kornilov-Kerensky State under which the working people of Russia have been suffering Kornilovism and Kerenskyism for half-a-year already. If the proletariat, if we have in mind a proletarian State—that is, the dictatorship of the proletariat—then the workers' control can become a national, all-embracing, universally realisable, most exact and most conscientious regulation of production and distribution of products.

Therein lies the chief difficulty, therein is the chief problem of the proletarian—that is, the Socialist revolution. Without the Soviets this problem, at any rate for Russia, would remain insoluble. The Soviets render possible that organising work of the proletariat which *can* solve this problem of world historical importance.

Here we have come to the other side of the question of the State machine. Besides the preponderatingly "repressive" part of the apparatus, the standing army, police, officialdom, there is in the contemporary State machine another part, closely interconnected with banks and syndicates, fulfilling a great mass of work of account-keeping and registration, if one may so express it. This part of the apparatus cannot and must not be broken up. It must only be torn from subjection to the capitalists. From it must be cut off, broken, chopped away the capitalists, with their wire-pulling influence. It must be *subjected* to the proletarian Soviets. It must be made wider, more all-embracing, more popular. And this can be done by basing our efforts on the achievements already attained by big capital (as, indeed, the proletarian revolution in general can only attain its aims by taking these achievements as its basis).

Capitalism created the apparatus for the keeping of accounts—*e.g.* the banks, syndicates, post, consumers' societies, unions of employees. *Without the big banks Socialism could not be realised.* The big banks form that State machine which we *need* for the realisation of Socialism and which we *take ready made* from capitalism. At the same time our problem here is to chop off that which capitalistically disfigures this otherwise excellect apparatus and to make it even *larger*, more democratic, more all-embracing. Quantity will pass over into quality. One State bank as huge as possible, with branches in every district, in every factory—this is already nine-tenths of the *Socialist* apparatus. This general State *account-keeping*—general State regulation of production and distribution of products—is, so to speak, something in the nature of the *skeleton* of socialist society. This "State apparatus" (which under capitalism is not wholly governmental but which will be completely governmental with us under Socialism) we can *take* over and "set into motion" at one blow, with one decree, because the actual work of account-keeping, control, registration, estimation and summation is here carried out by employees, most of whom are themselves in a proletarian or semi-proletarian position.

Will the Bolsheviks

The proletarian State can and must with one decree transform all the employees into State employees — in the same way that the watch-dogs of capitalism, such as Briand and other bourgeois ministers, transform striking railwaymen into the position of State servants. We shall need a great many more of such State employees; and more of them *can* be obtained, for capitalism has simplified the function of accounting and control and has brought them down to such comparatively simple processes as to be within the reach of any literate person.

The "nationalisation" of the bank, syndicate, commercial and other such employees is quite practicable technically (thanks to the preliminary work accomplished for us by capitalism and financial capitalism) and politically, under the conditions of the control and superintendence of the *Soviets*.

As for the higher employees, of whom there are very few, but who incline towards the capitalists, them we shall

have to treat like the capitalists—"with
severity." They, like the capitalists,
will *resist*. This resistance will have to
be *broken*, and although the never-to-be-
forgotten, naïve Peshechonov lisped as
long ago as June 19th, like a real State
schoolboy, that the resistance of the
capitalists had been broken, nevertheless what for him was a childish
phrase, a frivolous swagger, a mere
boyish sally, *will be accepted by the
proletariat in all seriousness*.

This we can do, for here it is merely
a question of breaking the resistance
of an insignificant minority of the
population, literally a handful of people,
over every one of whom the clerks'
unions, trade unions, consumers' societies and the Soviets will institute such
supervision that every man-jack of
them will be *surrounded* like the French
at Sedan. We know them all by name:
it is enough to take the lists of directors,
members of management boards, the
big shareholders, and so on. There are
a few hundreds of them, at most a **few**

thousands, in the whole of Russia, for each of whom the proletarian State, with its Soviet apparatus, its employees' unions and so on, can supply tens or hundreds of controllers, so that possibly, instead of "smashing the resistance," we may succeed, by means of the workers' control (over the capitalists), in making any *such resistance impossible.*

The vital matter is not the confiscation of capitalist property, but universal, all-embracing workers' control over the capitalists and their possible supporters. By means of confiscation alone one can do nothing, for in that there is no basis for organisation, or for the estimation of regular distribution. We shall readily substitute for confiscation the collection of just taxation (even in a Shingarev sense), if only we can thereby exclude the possibility of any sort of evasion of account rendering, concealing of the truth, or eluding the law. And only workers' control in the workers' State will remove this possibility.

Maintain Power ?

Forced syndicatisation—that is, forced fusion into unions under the control of the State—this is what capitalism has prepared for us—this is what the Banker State has realised in Germany —this is what will be completely realisable in Russia by the Soviets, by the dictatorship of the proletariat. This is what the State apparatus, universal, newest and non-bureaucratic, will give us. (For a more detailed description of the meaning of forced syndicatisation see my pamphlet, *The Threatening Catastrophe and How to Fight it.*)

V

THE fourth argument of the advocates of the bourgeoisie: the proletariat will be unable "to set in motion" the apparatus of government. This argument, in comparison with the third one, presents us with nothing new. The old apparatus we could neither seize nor set into motion. The new apparatus, the Soviets, have already been set into motion by the "mighty impulse of the real national creative genius." We need only free this apparatus from the shackles placed on it by the domination of the S.R. and Menshevik leaders. The apparatus is already in motion, it is only necessary to rid it of the disfiguring small bourgeois baubles which are hindering it from going forward and forward in full swing.

To complete what was said above, two

circumstances must be investigated:
first, the new methods of control that
have been created, not by us but by
capitalism in its military-imperialist
stage; second, the meaning of the
deepening and extension of democracy
in the work of administration of a
State of the proletarian type. The
bread monopoly and bread cards have
been instituted not by us but by
the belligerent capitalist State. It
has already created universal labour,
conscription within the framework of
capitalism—that is, a military penal
prison for the workers. But here too
the proletariat, as in all its historical
creative work, takes its implements
from capitalism, and does not "think
out" and "create things from nothing."

The bread monopoly, the bread cards,
universal labour and conscription become, in the hands of the proletarian
State, in the hands of the all-powerful
Soviets, one of the greatest means
for regulation and control, a means
which, extended to the capitalist and

the *rich in general*, being applied to them by the *workers*, will give a power so far unheard-of in history for the "setting in motion" of the apparatus of government, for the overcoming of the resistance of the capitalists, for their subjection to the proletarian State. This means of control and *compulsory labour* are stronger than the laws of the Convention and its guillotine. The guillotine only frightened, only crushed *active* resistance. *For us this is not enough.* We must not only frighten the capitalists so that they should feel the all-pervading strength of the proletarian State and should forget to think of active resistance to it. We must crush also their *passive* resistance, which is undoubtedly far more dangerous and harmful. We must not only crush every sort and kind of resistance. We have to *impose* work in the framework of the new State organisation. It is not enough to throw out the capitalists, it is necessary (after having kicked out the incapable

Maintain Power ?

unreliable "passive resisters") to put them to *new State service*. This applies to the capitalists as well as to a certain upper section of the bourgeois intellegentsia, clerks and so forth. And we have the means thereto. The belligerent capitalist State has itself given us the means and weapon whereby we can carry out this policy. This means is the bread monopoly, the bread cards, universal industrial conscription. "He who works not neither shall he eat." This is the basic, primary and chief rule which the Soviets of workers' deputies can and will bring into being as soon as they become the governing power. Every worker has an employment book. This document does not necessarily lower him, although at the present time it undoubtedly does form a document of capitalist wage slavery, testifying to the subjection of the working man to this or that parasite.

The Soviets will institute the employment book for the rich and then gradually for the whole population (in a peasant country an employment book will probably be unnecessary for a very long time for the overwhelming majority of the peasants). The employment book will cease to be a sign of belonging to the rabble, will cease to be a document of the "lower" orders, a certificate of wage-slavery. It will be converted into a witness of the fact that in the new society there are no longer any "labourers" but that, on the other hand, there is no one who is not a worker.

The rich must receive from that union of workers or clerks which is most nearly related to their sphere of activity an employment book. They must receive weekly, or at any other regular periods, a certificate from this union that they are doing their work conscientiously — without this they will not get their bread card or food products in general. We need good organisers in the banking business, and in the work of unifying various concerns (in these matters the capitalists have more experience, and work is done more easily with experienced people); we need more and more engineers, agriculturists, technicians, scientific experts of every kind. We shall give all such workers work in accordance with their strength and ability. Probably, we shall only gradually bring in equality for all work, leaving a temporary higher rate of pay for these specialists during that transition period, but we shall put them under a workers' control which will affect them on every side; we shall attain the full and unconditional application of the rule: "He who works not neither shall he eat." As for the form of organisation of the work, we do not simply think it out afresh ourselves, but we take it ready made from capitalism, from the banks, syndicates, the best factories, experimental stations, academies, and so forth. We need only adopt the best models furnished by the experience of the most

Will the Bolsheviks

progressive countries. And of course we shall not lose ourselves in a Utopia, we shall continue to look at things only in a sober, practical way; the whole capitalist class will manifest the most stubborn resistance, but by the organisation of the whole population in Soviets this resistance will be broken. At the same time, extra obstinate and non-submissive capitalists will of course have to be punished by the confiscation of the whole of their wealth and by imprisonment. On the other hand, the victory of the proletariat will increase the number of cases, about which, for instance, I read in to-day's "Isvestia":

"Sept. 26th, two engineers appeared before the Central Council of Factory and Workshop Committees with the declaration that the engineering group had decided to form a union of Socialist engineers. Considering that the present time is the beginning of social revolution, the union places itself at the disposal of the working masses, and, in the interests of the workers, it decides to act in complete unison with the workers' organisations. The representatives of the Central Council of Factory and Workshop Committees replied that the Council will gladly form within its organisation an engineering section including in its programme the fundamental thesis of the first conference of Factory and Workshop Committees regarding the workers' control over production. In the near future there will be a joint session of the delegates of the Central Council of Factory and Workshop Committees and the provisional group of Socialist engineers" ("Isvestia," September 27th, 1917).

The proletariat, we are told, will be unable to put the apparatus of government into motion.

After the 1905 revolution Russia was ruled by 130,000 landowners. They ruled by the exertion of unlimited force over 150,000,000 people, by means of pouring unlimited scorn on them, by means of subjecting the vast majority to penal labour and semi-starvation. And yet they tell us that Russia will not be able to be governed by the 240,000 members of the Bolshevik Party—governing in the interest of the poor and against the rich. These 240,000 already have no less than a million votes of the population behind them, for just this proportion of votes to members of the party has been ascertained from the experience in Europe and also in Russia, as, for instance, in the August municipal elections in Petrograd. So here we have already a "governing body" of a million, faithful to the ideal of the Socialist State, and not working merely for the sake of getting on every 20th of the month a considerable bundle of notes.

Moreover, we have a splendid means of increasing tenfold our apparatus of government—a means which never has been and never could be at the disposal of a capitalist State. It is a

very effective expedient: the drawing
in of the workers, the poor, to the daily
work of managing the State. To ex-
plain how simple is the application of
this splendid means, how faultless is
its action, we shall take the most
simple and evident example.

The State has forcibly to evict a
family from a house and to install
another in it. This is done times
without number by the capitalist
State, this will also have to be done
by ours, by the proletarian or Socialist
State.

The capitalist State turns out of its
home a workers' family which has lost
its breadwinner and does not pay rent.
There comes upon the scene a bailiff,
policeman, or military officer, a whole
platoon of men. In a working-class
district a whole detachment of Cossacks
is necessary for the eviction. Why?
Because the bailiff and police refuse
to go without a military protection
of considerable strength. They know
that the scene of an eviction induces

such mad fury among the neighbouring population, driven in thousands and thousands well-nigh to despair, such hatred against the capitalists and the capitalist State, that the bailiff and the squad of police might at any moment be torn to pieces. Huge military force is necessary. Several regiments of soldiers must be brought into the town from a necessarily distant province, so that the soldiers might know nothing of the poverty of the townspeople, so that the soldiers might not be "infected" with Socialism.

Now suppose the proletarian State has forcibly to move a very needy family into the dwelling of a rich man. Our detachment of workers' militia consists, let us say, of fifteen people—two sailors, two soldiers, two class-conscious workers (of which let perhaps only one be a member of our party or sympathising with it), then one from the intelligentsia, and eight poor labourers, of whom there would

Maintain Power?

be at least five women, servants, common workmen, and so on. The detachment comes to the rich man's house, investigates, and finds five rooms for two men and two women. "For this winter, citizens, you must confine yourselves to two rooms and prepare two rooms for the reception of two families who are now living in cellars. For a time, until with the help of engineers (you are an engineer, I think?) we construct good houses for all, you will have to put yourselves out a bit. Your telephone will serve ten families. This will economise about a hundred hours' work in running about, and so on. Then in your family there are two unoccupied semi-workers capable of doing light work —a woman citizen of fifty-five and a boy of fourteen. They will be on duty for three hours daily, superintending the distribution of products for the ten families and they will keep the necessary accounts. The student in our detachment will write out two copies of the text of this State order and you will kindly give us a signed declaration of your undertaking to carry out the duties accurately." Thus, in my view, could be compared in very evident examples the nature and administration of the old bourgeois and the new Socialist State apparatus.

We are not Utopians. We know that just any labourer or any cook would be incapable of taking over immediately the administration of the State. In this we agree with the Cadets, with Breshkovskaia, and with Tseretelli. But we are distinguished from these citizens in that we demand a break away from the prejudice that assumes that the *administration* of the State, the performance of the ordinary, everyday work of management, can only be done by the rich or by officials taken from rich families. We demand that the teaching of the business of government should be conducted by the class-conscious workers and soldiers, that this should be started immediately

Maintain Power?

—that is, that all the labouring masses, all the poverty-stricken, should immediately start receiving this instruction. We know that the Cadets are also agreeable to the teaching of democracy to the people. Cadet ladies are willing to give lectures to servants on women's rights, in accordance with the best French and English authorities. Also, at the very next concert meeting, before an audience of thousands of people, there will be arranged on the platform a general kissing. A Cadet lady lecturer will kiss Breshkovskaia. The latter will kiss the former minister Tseretelli. And a grateful people will thus learn the meaning of republican equality, liberty and fraternity. . . .

Yes, we quite agree that Breshkovskaia and Tseretelli are in their own way devoted to democracy, and propagate it amongst the people; but what is to be done if we have a somewhat different idea of democracy from theirs?

According to us, in order to mitigate

the unheard-of burdens and misfortunes of the war, and at the same time to heal the terrible wounds inflicted on the people by the war, *revolutionary* democracy is necessary, *revolutionary* measures are needed, exactly of the kind described in the example of the redistribution of dwellings in the interests of the poor. *Exactly in the same way* must we deal both in town and country with foodstuffs, clothes, boots, and so on, and in the country with the landowners' land and so forth. For the administration of the State in spirit we can bring into action *immediately an administrative machine* of about ten if not twenty millions—an apparatus unknown in any capitalist country. Only *we* are capable of creating such an apparatus, for we are assured of the full unlimited sympathy of the vast majority of the population. This apparatus only *we* can create, because we have conscious workers, disciplined by a long "apprenticeship" to capitalism (not for naught did we serve this apprenticeship to capitalism), workers who are *capable* of forming a workers' militia and *gradually* of enlarging it (commencing this enlargement immediately) into a *universal* militia. The conscious workers must be in control, but they can attract to the actual work of management the real labouring and oppressed masses.

Of course, mistakes are inevitable during the first activities of this new apparatus.

But did the peasants make no mistakes when they first threw off the shackles of serfdom and, becoming free, began to manage their own affairs? Can there be any other method of teaching the people to manage their own affairs and to avoid mistakes than that of actual practice, than the immediate starting of real popular self-administration? The most important thing at the present time is to get rid of the prejudice of the bourgeois intelligentsia that only special officials, entirely dependent on capital by their whole social position, can carry on the administration of the State. The most important thing is to put an end to that state of affairs in which officials and "Socialist" ministers try to manage the State in accordance with the old bourgeois methods; they simply cannot manage properly, and, after seven months, are faced with peasant risings in a peasant State. The most important thing is to instil in the oppressed and labouring masses confidence in their own power, to show them by actual practice that they can and must themselves undertake regular, most strict, orderly, organised distribution of bread, of every kind of food, milk, clothing, dwellings and so on, in the interests of the poorest. Without this there can be no salvation of Russia from collapse and ruin; whereas an honest, courageous, universal first move to hand over the management of the country to the proletariat and semi-proletariat will cause such an unheard-of revolutionary enthusiasm in the masses, will multiply so many times the popular forces in the struggle with our misfortunes, that much that seemed impossible to our narrow old bureaucratic forces will become practicable for the million-numbered masses, beginning to work for themselves and not for the capitalist, not for a boss or official and not under compulsion of the stick.

VI

TOGETHER with the question of the apparatus of government we must take the question of centralism, raised in a particularly energetic, but particularly unsuccessful, manner by Comrade Basarov in No. 138 of the *Novaya Zhizhn*, September 27th, in the article, "The Bolsheviks and the Problem of Power."

Comrade Basarov reasons thus: The Soviets are not the kind of apparatus applicable to all spheres of State life, for a seven months' trial is supposed to have shown, and the evidence of "tens and hundreds of documents possessed by the economic section of the Petrograd Executive Committee" to have confirmed, that although in many places the Soviets have had practically "full control," "they could not obtain any sort of satisfactory results

The Bolsheviks

in their campaign against the ravaged state of the country." It is necessary to have an apparatus "divided according to branches of industry strictly centralised within the limits of each branch and subject to one general State centre." "It is a question"—kindly note—"not of a replacement of the old apparatus, but of its reformation, . . . however much the Bolsheviks may sneer at people with plans."

All these observations of Comrade Basarov are really amazingly helpless. They are an exact copy of the bourgeois mode of discussion—a reflection of its class point of view.

Now, really, to speak of the Soviets as having had anywhere in Russia, at any time, "full power" is simply absurd (if it is not a mere repetition of the interested class lies of the capitalists). Full power means power over the whole land, over all the banks, all the factories. A man but slightly acquainted with historical experience, with scientific facts of the connection of politics with economics, could not "forget" this "slight" circumstance.

The lie in the measures adopted by the bourgeoisie consists in this, that, refusing to give the Soviets power, *sabotaging* every one of their serious attempts, preserving the government in their own hands, maintaining their hold on the land and banks and so on, they yet throw all the blame for the ruin of the country on the Soviets! And just this lies at the bottom of the whole policy of the Coalition.

The Soviets never had full power, and their measures so far could yield nothing but palliatives and further entanglements.

To prove to the Bolsheviks, convinced centralists as they are by programme and the tactics of the whole of their party, the need for centralism, is in very truth a hammering at open doors. If the writers of the *Novaya Zhizhn* occupy themselves with such absurdities, it is only because they have completely misunderstood the meaning of

Maintain Power ?

our jokes regarding their "State as a whole" point of view. And they did not understand this because the *Novaya Zhizhnists* only recognise the class war with their *lips*, not with their brains. Repeating the words about the class struggle which they have learnt by heart, they stumble every second over the interesting, theoretical, reactionary, practical, "above-class point of view," calling this servility to the bourgeoisie a general State plan. The State, my dear people, is a class idea. The State is an organ or machine for the subjection of one class by another; so long as it remains a machine for the dominance of the bourgeoisie over the proletariat, so long must the cry of the latter be— the *destruction* of this State. But when the State has become proletarian, when it has become a machine for the domination of the proletariat over the bourgeoisie, then we shall be fully and unreservedly for a strong government and centralism. Speaking more

Will the Bolsheviks

popularly, we are not ridiculing plans, we only laugh at the fact that Basarov and Company do not understand that, in rejecting "workers' control," in denying the dictatorship of the proletariat, they *stand for* the dictatorship of the bourgeoisie. There is no midway. The latter is but an empty dream of the petty bourgeois democrat. Not a single central organ, not a single Bolshevik ever disputed the need for the centralisation of the Soviets or the need for their unification. None of us has ever said anything against the organisation of factory and workshop committees by branches of production and their centralisation. Basarov is simply shooting *beside the mark*. We laugh, have laughed, and shall continue to laugh, not at centralisation, nor at plans, but at mere *reformism*. For your reformist is doubly comical after the experience of the Coalition. And to say: "Not the replacement of the machine but its reform" is to show that one is reformist, that one is becoming not a revolutionary but a reformist democrat. Reformism is nothing more than the granting of concessions whilst preserving power in one's own hands. This is exactly what has been tried by the Coalition for half-a-year.

This is just what we are ridiculing. Basarov, not having thought out the idea of the class war, allows himself to be caught by the bourgeoisie, which sings in chorus: "Just—just so—we are not at all against reform, we are in favour of the participation of the workers in the control of the State as a whole, we are quite in agreement," and the good Basarov plays *objectively* the rôle of repeating echo to the capitalists.

This has always been and always will be the case with people who, in times of acute class struggle, endeavour to occupy a "midway" position. And it is just because the writers of the *Novaya Zhizhn* are incapable of understanding the class war that their policy is so ridiculous — a continuous wobbling between the bourgeoisie and the proletariat.

Take to plan-making by all means, my dear citizens—that is not politics, it is not a matter of the class war. In this sphere you can indeed be useful to the people. You have many economists on your paper; unite with such engineers as are ready to work a little on the question of the regulation of production and distribution. Give up the deposit list of your huge apparatus (your paper) for a business-like working out of exact details regarding the production and distribution of products in Russia, regarding the banks, syndicates, and so on and so on. Herein you will benefit the people. Herein your position between two stools can do no great harm. Here is work on "plans" which will arouse, not the ridicule, but the gratitude of the workers.

The proletariat, when victorious, will act thus. It will set the economists, engineers, agricultural experts and so on to work out plans under the control of the workers' organisations, to test these plans, to seek means of economising labour by centralisation, and of securing the most simple, cheap, convenient, general control. We shall pay the economists, statisticians, technicians; for all this there will be good money, but—but we shall not give them anything to eat unless they carry out this work honestly and entirely in *the interests of the workers.*

We are in favour of centralisation and of plans, but it must be the centralisation and the plans of the *proletarian State*—the proletarian regulation of production and distribution in the interests of the poor, the labouring, the exploited, *against* the exploiters. By "the State as a whole" we agree to understand only that which will break the resistance of the capitalists, which will give the whole power to the majority of the people—that is, to the proletariat, the semi-proletariat, and the poorest peasantry.

VII

THE fifth argument is that the Bolsheviks will be unable to retain power because "the circumstances are exceptionally complicated."

Oh, what wiseacres! they are prepared perhaps to tolerate revolution, but without "exceptionally complicated circumstances."

Such revolutions never occur. And in the yearnings after such revolutions there is nothing but the reactionary lamentation of the educated bourgeois. Even if a revolution were to start in circumstances which seemed not so very complicated, the revolution itself, in its development, would give rise to exceptionally complicated circumstances. For a revolution, a real, deep, "people's revolution," to use the expression of Marx, is an incredibly complicated and painful process, in-

The Bolsheviks

volving the dying of the old and the birth of the new social order, and the refashioning of the lives of tens of millions of people. Revolution is the sharpest, most furious, desperate class war and civil war. Not a single great revolution in history has escaped civil war. No one who does not live in a shell could imagine that civil war is conceivable without exceptionally complicated circumstances. If there were no exceptionally complicated circumstances there would be no revolution. If you fear wolves—do not go into the forest.

In this fifth argument there is nothing to discuss, because there is neither economic nor political nor indeed any kind of index at all behind it. It is only the groaning of people who have been made unhappy and frightened by the revolution. To characterise these groans, I shall take the liberty of recalling two slight personal reminiscences.

I talked with a rich engineer not

long before the July days. The engineer was at one time a revolutionary, a member of the Social-Democratic, indeed of the Bolshevik party. Now he is just in one tremor of fear and fury at the turbulent, untamable workers. "If at least they were workers, like the Germans," said he (an educated man who had been on the Continent), "I of course would understand the inevitability, in a general way, of the social revolution, but here at the low level of the workers induced by the war . . . it is not revolution, it is catastrophe."

He would be prepared to welcome the revolution if history would lead up to it in the same peaceful, quiet, smooth, orderly way in which one goes up to a German passenger train, where a decorous conductor opens the door of the carriage and calls out: "Social Revolution Station! All change!" In such a case, why should one not pass over from the position of engineer under the bourgeoisie to that of engineer under the workers' organisation?

This man had seen a strike, he knew what a flood of passion is always aroused by an ordinary strike, even in the most peaceful times. He is bound, of course, to understand how many million times stronger must this storm be when the class struggle has aroused the whole labouring people of a great nation, when the war and exploitation has reduced well-nigh to despair millions of people who have been tortured for centuries by landowners, and who have been robbed and downtrodden for tens of years by the capitalists and Tsarist officials. He understands all this "theoretically." He recognises all this with his lips. He has simply been scared by the "exceptionally complicated circumstances."

After the July days I was compelled, on account of the specially anxious attention paid me by Kerensky's government, to go underground. Of course it was the workers who gave us shelter.

Will the Bolsheviks

In an out-of-the-way workers' suburb of Petrograd, in a small working-class house, dinner is being served. The hostess puts bread on the table. "Look," says the host, "what fine bread. They dare not give us bad bread. And to think that good bread could be had in Petrograd at one time!"

I was amazed at this class valuation of the July days. My ideas had revolved around the political significance of the revolution, estimated its rôle in the general course of events, analysed the development of the situation that had given rise to the zigzag and its further developments, and considered how we must alter our battle-cries and party machine so as to adapt it to the changed circumstances. As for bread I, who had never been in need, never thought at all. Bread to me appeared as it were of itself, as a sort of by-product of writing work. Through political analysis, one's ideas reached, by an extraordinarily complicated and involved path, the basis of all, the class struggle for bread.

But the representative of the oppressed class, although one of the well-paid and well-educated workers, takes the bull straight by the horns, with that wonderful simplicity and directness, with that firm determination, with that astonishing clear insight, which is as far from us, the intelligentsia, as the stars in the sky. The whole world is divided into two camps. "We," the labouring, and "They," the exploiters. Not a shade of agitation regarding the past—just one of the battles in the long struggle of labour against capital. The wood is being cut down; the chips fly. What a painful thing is this " exceptionally complicated circumstances " of the revolution ! Thus thinks and feels the educated bourgeois. We have screwed "them" down. "They" will not dare to chide as before. Let us press "them" harder still, let us overthrow them altogether ! Thus thinks and feels the worker.

VIII

THE sixth and last argument is that the proletariat will be "incapable of withstanding the whole pressure of hostile forces, which will sweep away not only the dictatorship of the proletariat but in addition the whole revolution."

Do not try to scare us; we shall not be scared. We have seen these hostile forces and their pressure in Kornilovism (from which Kerenskyism differs in no way). How daring were the proletariat and the poorest peasantry against Kornilovism: how pitiful and helpless was the position of the supporters of the bourgeoisie and the small number of representatives of the specially well-to-do small local landowners, particularly hostile to the revolution. These things were seen by all; they are remembered by the people. The *Dielo*

The Bolsheviks

Naroda of September 30th, in trying to persuade the workers to "tolerate" Kerenskyism—that is, Kornilovism—and Tseretelli's fake Bulygin Duma until the summoning of the Constituent Assembly (summoned under the protection of "military measures" against the rebelling peasants!), repeats, choking, this sixth argument of the *Novaya Zhizhn*, and screams till it becomes hoarse: "Kerensky's Government will under no circumstances give in" (to the Soviet power, to the power of the workers and peasants, which, not to lag behind the Black Hundreds, the anti-Semites, Monarchists and Cadets, the *Dielo Naroda* calls the power of Trotsky and Lenin—thus low have the S.R.'s sunk!).

But the conscious workers are not to be frightened either by the *Dielo Naroda* or by the *Novaya Zhizhn*. "Kerensky's Government," you say, "will under no circumstances give in" —that is, they will repeat Kornilovism, to speak more simply, more directly, more clearly. And the gentlemen of the *Dielo Naroda* dare to say that that will be "civil war," that this is a "terrible prospect." No, gentlemen, you will not deceive the workers. This will not be a civil war, but a most hopeless conspiracy of a handful of Kornilovists: or perhaps they wish, by not "giving in" to the people, at all costs to provoke a repetition on a large scale of what happened at Viborg in connection with the Kornilovists. If the S.R.'s *desire* this, if the member of the S.R. party, Kerensky, desires this, you can drive the people to delirium, but you will not frighten the workers and soldiers, gentlemen.

What unlimited impudence! They fake a new Bulygin Duma by means of trickery, they whip up a crowd of reactionary co-operators to their assistance, and also a number of country kulaks; they add to these some capitalists and landowners (called propertied elements): and this band of Kornilovists they want to *set free* from subjection to

the *will of the people*, the will of the
workers and peasants.

They have reduced a peasant land to
such a condition that everywhere, on
all sides, there are peasants' risings!
Just think of it! In a democratic
republic, containing 80 per cent. of
peasants, there are actually peasants'
risings. . . . The same *Dielo Naroda*,
Tchernov's organ, the organ of the
party of Socialist - Revolutionaries,
which, on September 30th, has the
shamelessness to advise the workers
and peasants to "endure," was forced
to admit, in a leading article on September 29th, that "almost nothing has
so far been done to destroy the *servile*
relations which *still reign supreme* in
the villages of Central Russia."

This same *Dielo Naroda*, in the
same leader, September 29th, says that
"the customs of Stolypin still allow
themselves to be felt strongly in
the measures of the 'revolutionary
ministers.'" That is, in other words they
call Kerensky, Nikitin, Kishkin and

Will the Bolsheviks

Co., Stolypinists. The "Stolypinists" Kerensky and Co. have brought the peasantry to rebellion, and now they introduce "military measures" against the peasantry, and console the nation with promises to summon the Constituent Assembly (although Kerensky and Tseretelli have already *deceived* the nation once, for, after triumphantly declaring, on July 8th, that the Constituent Assembly would be called together on September 17th, they *broke their word* and put off the Constituent Assembly, even against the advice of the *Menshevik Dan*, not to the end of October as the Menshevik Central Executive Committee of that time desired, but to the end of November). The "Stolypinists" Kerensky and Co. console the people with the idea of the early convocation of the Constituent Assembly, as though the people could trust those who have already played them false in like circumstances, as though the people could believe in the honest summoning of the Constituent Assembly by a government which is introducing *military measures* in out-of-the-way villages, and thus quite evidently *concealing* arbitrary arrests of class-conscious peasants and the *falsification* of the elections. They drive the peasants to revolt, and then have the impudence to tell them that it is necessary to "endure," it is necessary to wait a while, to trust that government which is putting down the revolting peasants with "military measures"! They bring matters to such a pass as to drive to perdition hundreds of thousands of Russian soldiers in the assault after June 19th, to prolong the war, to provoke the rising of the German sailors, who threw their superiors overboard, they bring about such a state of affairs, all the time uttering fine phrases about peace, *without offering* a just peace to all the belligerent nations. And yet they have the effrontery to tell the workers and peasants, to tell the dying soldiers —"You must endure a bit, trust

Will the Bolsheviks

the government of the 'Stolypinist' Kerensky, have faith another month in the Kornilovist generals (who perhaps in another month will lead to the slaughter a few more tens of thousands of soldiers) . . . forbear a little longer." Is this not impudence?

No, Messieurs S.R.'s—party colleagues of Kerensky—you will not deceive the soldiers.

Not one day, not one extra hour, will the workers and soldiers tolerate the Kerensky government, for they know that the Soviet government will make an immediate offer of a just peace to all the combatants, and will therefore in all probability obtain an immediate armistice and an early peace. Not a day, not an hour longer than *possible*, will the soldiers of our peasant army tolerate that, in spite of the opposition of the Soviets, there should remain the Kerensky government with its *military measures* for putting down the peasant risings. No, Messieurs S.R.'s—party colleagues of Kerensky — you will no longer deceive the workers and peasants.

In the question of the pressure of the hostile forces, which, according to the assurances of the terrified *Novaya Zhizhn*, will sweep away the dictatorship of the proletariat, there is another marvellous logical and political error which only those can pass over who have allowed themselves to be terrorised to the point of irresponsibility.

"The pressure of hostile forces," you say, "will sweep away the dictatorship of the proletariat." Very well. But you are all economists and educated people, my dear fellow-citizens. You all know that to compare democracy with the bourgeoisie is senseless and clownish, that it is just the same as comparing poods (measure of weight) to arshins (measure of length). For there are democratic bourgeoisie and non-democratic (capable of Vendeeism) sections of the petty bourgeoisie.

"Hostile forces"—that is a phrase. The class meaning of it, however, is the *bourgeoisie* (in support of which also stand the landowners).

The bourgeoisie, and the landowners; the proletariat; the petty bourgeoisie, the small owners amongst whom first come the peasants—there are three fundamental "forces" into which Russia is divided like *every* capitalist country. Here are the three fundamental "forces" which are made evident in every capitalist country (and in Russia) not only by an economic analysis but by the *political experience* of all the more recent history of all countries, by the experience of all European revolutions of the eighteenth century, and by the experience of the two Russian revolutions of 1905 and 1917.

And so you threaten the proletariat that the pressure of the bourgeoisie will sweep away their power? This and this only is what your threat comes to; it has no other meaning. Very well. If really the bourgeoisie can sweep away the power of the workers and poorest peasantry, then

nothing else remains than "Coalition"—
that is, a union or understanding of the
petty bourgeoisie with the bourgeoisie.
Nothing else can even be imagined.

But the Coalition has been tried for
half-a-year, and has led to a crash, and
you yourselves, citizens of the *Novaya
Zhizhn*, who think clearly, though feebly,
you yourselves have *forsworn* it.

So what do we get?

You have become so muddled, citizens
of the *Novaya Zhizhn*. You have allowed
yourselves to be so scared that even in
the most simple discussion, in a summing
up, not even of five but only of three,
you cannot make your ends meet.

Either all power to the bourgeoisie—
this you have not defended for a long
time, indeed not even the bourgeoisie
itself dares to hint at it, knowing that
already on April 20th–21st the people
overthrew such a power by one motion
of their shoulder, and would overthrow
it now thrice as determinedly and merci-
lessly. Or all power to the petty bourgeoisie—that is, to its coalition (union,

understanding) with the bourgeoisie, for the petty bourgeoisie cannot and does not wish to take power independently; this has been proved by the experience of all revolutions; it is also proved by economic science, which explains that in a capitalist country one can stand for capitalism or for labour but one cannot keep on one's feet midway. Such a coalition in Russia has attempted dozens of methods for half-a-year, and has failed. Or, finally, the proletariat and poorest peasantry must assume full power against the bourgeoisie in order to break its resistance. This has not yet been tried, and this you, gentlemen of the *Novaya Zhizhn*, are dissuading the people from doing, trying to infect them with your own fear of the bourgeoisie. No fourth course can be thought out at all.

Consequently if the *Novaya Zhizhn* is afraid of the dictatorship of the proletariat, and sagely rejects it because of the possible defeat of a proletarian authority by the bourgeoisie, then this

Maintain Power ?

amounts to a stealthy return to the position of an *understanding* with the capitalists ! ! ! It is as clear as daylight that he who is afraid of resistance, who does not believe in the possibility of breaking this resistance, he who admonishes the people: "Take heed of the resistance of the capitalists, you will be unable to overcome it," *thereby* invokes again the acceptance of an understanding with the capitalists.

How helpless and pitiful is the confusion of the *Novaya Zhizhn,* as also now that of the petty bourgeois democrats who see the crash of the Coalition, but dare not defend it openly, while, being themselves protected by the bourgeoisie, they are afraid of an all-powerful proletariat and poorest peasantry.

To be afraid of the resistance of the capitalists while calling oneself a revolutionary and desiring to be numbered amongst the Socialists—what a disgrace! What an intellectual fall of international Socialism, corrupted by opportunism, was necessary that such voices could appear!

We have already seen, the whole nation has already seen, the strength of the capitalist resistance: for the capitalists, being more class-conscious than the other classes, at once recognised the meaning of the Soviets, and immediately spent every bit of their strength, did all and everything, adopted every device, went to the length of most atrocious measures of lies and abuse, of military plots—all in order to overthrow the Soviets, to reduce their power to *nil*, to prostitute them (with the help of the S.R.'s and Mensheviks), to transform them into talking shops, and to tire out the peasants and workers by months and months of idle speechmaking and playing at revolution.

But the strength of the resistance of the proletariat and poorest peasantry we have as yet not seen, for this strength will be exerted fully only when full power is in the hands of

the proletariat, when tens of millions
of people crushed by need and capitalist
slavery will see by actual experience,
will *feel*, that power in the State has
really been attained by the oppressed
classes, that the holders of this power
are really helping poverty, are strug-
gling with the landowners and capitalists, are *breaking* their resistance. Only
then shall we be able to see what un-
tapped forces of resistance to capitalism
are hidden within the people, only then
will be made evident what Engels calls
"hidden Socialism." Only then will it
appear that for every ten thousand
open or concealed enemies who resist,
actively or passively, the authority of
the working class, *a million* new fighters
arise, until then politically slumbering;
chilled by the tortures of poverty, in
despair, having lost belief in their own
manhood, having forgotten that they
too have a right to live, that they too
could serve the modern centralised
State, that they too could serve as
proletarian militia, with full responsi-

bility in immediate, direct, daily participation in the work of administration of the State.

The capitalists and landowners, with the sympathetic help of the Messieurs Plekhanovs, Breshkovskaias, Tseretellis, Tchernovs and Company, have done *everything* to *soil* the democratic Republic, to pollute it by their servility to wealth, to such an extent that the people have been seized by apathy and indifference. It is *all the same* to them, for a hungry man cannot distinguish between a Republic and a Monarchy: a frozen, shoeless, weary soldier, perishing for the interests of others, is incapable of getting to love a Republic. However, when the last common workman, every unemployed, every cook, every ruined peasant sees, not from the paper, but with his own eyes, that the proletarian authority is not cringing before the rich, but is helping poverty, that this power is not afraid of revolutionary measures, that it takes surplus products from the parasites and gives

them to the hungry, that it forcibly
moves the homeless into the dwellings
of the rich, that it forces the rich to pay
for milk, but does not give them a drop
of it until the children of *all* the poor
families have received adequate sup-
plies, that the land is passing into the
hands of those who labour on it, that
the factories and banks come under
the control of the workers, that serious
and immediate punishment is meted
out to millionaires who conceal their
riches—when the poverty-stricken see
and feel this, then no force of the
capitalists and kulaks, no forces supported by the hundreds of milliards
of international financial capital, will
be able to conquer the people's revolution. On the contrary, *it* will conquer
the whole world, for in all countries
the Socialist transformation is ripening;
our revolution is unconquerable if it is
not afraid of itself, if it entrusts full
authority to the proletariat. For on
our side stand the still immeasurably
huge, more developed, more organised

Will the Bolsheviks

world forces of the proletariat, temporarily crushed by the war, but not destroyed; on the contrary, only multiplied by it.

To fear that the power of the Bolsheviks—that is, the power of the proletariat, which is assured of the unlimited support of the poorest peasantry—will be "swept away" by the capitalists, gentlemen! What short-sightedness! What disgraceful distrust of the people! What hypocrisy! The people who manifest this fear belong to that "upper" (by capitalist standards, but in reality *rotten*) "society," which pronounces the word "justice" without themselves believing in it, as a habit, as a phrase without putting any content into it.

Here is an example: Mr Peshechonov is a well-known semi-Cadet; a more moderate labour man, at one in ideas with the Breshkovskaias and Plekhanovs, it would be difficult to find; there was no minister more servile to the bourgeoisie; the world has never seen a warmer partisan of the "Coalition," of an understanding with the capitalists. This is the kind of admission that this gentleman was compelled to make in his speech at the Democratic (read Bulygin) convention, according to the report of the patriotic Isvestia:

"There are two programmes. One is the programme of the claims made by a group—namely, class and national pretensions. This programme is most candidly defended by the Bolsheviks. But the other sections of the democracy cannot readily reject this programme. For this is a recognition of the claims of the labouring masses, of the ill-treated and oppressed nationalities. It is not so easy, therefore, for the democracy to break with the Bolsheviks, to deny these class demands, above all because these demands are, in their essence, just. But this programme for which we struggled before the revolution, for the sake of which we made the revolution, and

Will the Bolsheviks

which under other circumstances we should all have supported very amicably, presents, under present circumstances, a great danger. The danger is now so much the greater that these demands have to be asserted at a moment when their satisfaction by the State is impossible. We must first of all save the whole—the State—we must first of all save it from ruin, and there is only one way of doing this, to refuse to satisfy demands, however just and strong they might appear, and instead to call for limitations and sacrifices, which must be practised on all sides" ("Isvestia" of the Central Executive Committee, September 17th).

Mr Peshechonov does not understand that, whilst the capitalists are in power, he is defending not the interests of the whole of Russia but the avaricious interests of Russian and "Allied" imperialist capital. Mr Peshechonov does not understand that the war will cease to be an imperialist, predatory war of conquest only after a break with the

Maintain Power?

capitalists, with their secret treaties,
with their annexations (their seizure
of others' lands), with their banking
financial swindles. Mr Peshechonov
does not understand that only after this
would the war become—if the enemy
were to reject a formal offer of a
just peace—a defensive just war. Mr
Peshechonov does not understand that
the defensive power of the country,
after ridding itself of the yoke of
capitalism, and after giving the land to
the peasants and placing the banks and
factories under workers' control, would
be many times stronger than the defensive power of a capitalist country.

And, most important of all, Mr
Peshechonov does not understand that
when he is forced to admit the justice
of Bolshevism, to admit that its demands are the demands of the labouring masses—that is, of the majority of
the nation—he abandons thereby his
whole position, the whole position of
the petty bourgeois democracy. Herein
exactly lies our strength. Our govern-

ment will be unconquerable because
even our antagonists are forced to
admit that the Bolshevik programme
is the programme of the "labouring
masses" and "oppressed nationalities."

Mr Peshechonov is, remember, the
political friend of the Cadets, of
the people of the *Yedinstvo* and the
Dielo Naroda, of the Breshkovskaias
of the Plekhanovs. He is the representative of the kulaks and of those
gentlemen whose wives and sisters
would come to-morrow to poke out
the eyes of the dying Bolsheviks, if
it came to their being beaten by
Kornilov's or (what comes exactly to
the same thing) by Kerensky's soldiers.
And such a gentleman is *compelled* to
recognise the justice of the Bolshevik
demands. For him "justice" is but a
phrase. But for the masses of the
semi-proletariat, for the majority of
the petty bourgeoisie of town and
country, ruined, exhausted, tortured
by the war, it is not a phrase, but a
most direct and most burning question,

the biggest question of all, deciding whether they will die by starvation or receive their crust of bread. This is why no policy can be based on "Coalition," on "agreement" of the interests of the hungry and ruined with the interests of the exploiters. This is why the Bolshevik government is assured of the support of the overwhelming majority of these masses. Justice is an empty word, say the intelligentsia, and those rascals who are inclined to declare themselves Marxists on the very dignified ground that they have once contemplated the back door of "economic materialism."

An idea becomes a power when it seizes hold of the masses; and just now the Bolsheviks—that is, the representatives of revolutionary proletarian internationalism—have by their policy given life to this idea which is stirring the vast labouring masses of the whole world. Justice of itself, the mere feelings of the indignant exploited masses, would never have led them on the right

The Bolsheviks

road to Socialism. But when, thanks
to capitalism, there grew up the apparatus of big banks, syndicates, railways,
and so on, when the rich experience
of the most advanced countries has
amassed a hoard of marvellous technical knowledge the application of which
capitalism is now *hindering*, when the
conscious workers have formed a party
of a quarter of a million, for the purpose of taking this apparatus into their
hands in an orderly fashion, and setting it going with the support of all the
labouring and exploited—when these
conditions are evident to all, then
there is no force on earth which can
hinder the Bolsheviks, if only they do
not allow themselves to be cowed and
are able to seize power, from also retaining it until the final victory of the
world Socialist Revolution.

AN AFTERWORD

THE foregoing lines had already been
written when the leader of the *Novaya
Zhizhn* of October 1st threw up a new
pearl of stupidity, the more dangerous
since it is concealed under the flag of
sympathy for the Bolsheviks, or under
the shelter of the most wise philistine
discussion. "Not to let ourselves be
provoked" (not to let ourselves be
caught in a snare of screams about
provocation serving the purpose of
frightening off the Bolsheviks from
seizing power).

Here is this pearl:

"The lessons of movements such as
those on July 3rd and 5th, on the one
hand, and the Kornilov days on the
other, have shown quite clearly that
the democracy which has at its disposal
the most influential sections of the
population is invincible when it is on

the defensive in a civil war, but that
it suffers defeat, losing all the intermediate vacillating elements, when it
takes the offensive initiative into its
own hands."

If the Bolsheviks were to show in
any form whatever any leanings towards the kind of philistine stupidity
expressed in this argument they would
ruin both their party and the revolution. For the author of this argument,
having taken it upon himself to talk of
civil war (a theme very suitable indeed
for that perfectly charming lady, the
Novaya Zhizhn), has perverted the *lessons
of history* with an almost incredibly
comic result.

Here is how the representative and
founder of the art of proletarian revolutionary tactics discussed these
lessons, the lessons of history, on this
question.

"Insurrection is an art just as is war
or any other form of art. It is subject
to certain rules, the non-observance of

which leads to the ruin of the party
which is to blame for neglecting them.
These rules, being logical deductions
from the nature of these parties and
from the circumstances with which one
has to deal in such a case, are so simple
that the short experience of 1848 had
made the Germans pretty well acquainted with them. Firstly, never
play with insurrection if there is no
determination to drive it to the bitter
end (literally—to face all the conse-
quences of this play). An insurrection
is an equation with very indefinite
magnitudes, the value of which may
change every day. The forces to be
opposed have all the advantages of
organisation, discipline and traditional
authority." (Marx has in mind the most
difficult case of insurrection against a
"firmly established" old Power, against
an army that had not yet decayed under
the influence of the revolution and the
vacillating policy of the government.)
"If the rebels cannot bring great
forces to bear against their antagonists,

they will be smashed and destroyed. Secondly, the insurrection once started, it is necessary to act with the utmost determination and pass over to the offensive. The defensive is the death of every armed rising; it perishes before it has measured forces with the enemy. The antagonists must be surprised while their soldiers are still scattered, and new successes, however small, must be attained daily; the moral ascendancy given by the first successes of the rising must be kept up. One must rally to the side of the insurrection the vacillating elements, which always follow the stronger, and which always look out for the safer side. Force your enemies to retreat before they can collect their forces against you. In one word, act according to the words of Danton—the greatest master of revolutionary policy yet known — 'Audacity, audacity and yet again audacity !' " (*Revolution and Counter Revolution*, German Edition, 1907, p. 18).

Maintain Power ?

We have altered all this, the "also Marxists" of the *Novaya Zhizhn* might say of themselves: instead of triple audacity we have two qualities—yes, we have two—"moderation and punctiliousness." For "us" the experience of world history, the experience of the great French Revolution, is of no consequence. For us the experience of the two movements of 1917, distorted by Molchalin spectacles, is sufficient.

Let us have a look at this experience without these fine spectacles.

July 3rd–5th you compare with "civil war"; for you implicitly believe Alexinsky, Pereverzev and Company. It is characteristic of the gentlemen of the *Novaya Zhizhn* that they believe *such* people (while doing nothing themselves independently to *collect* information regarding July 3rd–5th, in spite of the big apparatus of their daily journal).

But let us concede for a moment that July 3rd–5th was not merely an incident in the civil war, kept by the Bolsheviks within the limits of a mere incident, but a real civil war—let us grant this. What then does this lesson indicate?

Firstly, that the Bolsheviks did *not* take the offensive, for it is indisputable that had they taken the offensive on the night of July 3rd–4th, and even during July 4th, they would have achieved a good deal. Their defensive tactics were their weakness, if we are to talk of a civil war (as does the *Novaya Zhizhn*) and not of the transformation of an elemental explosion into a demonstration of the type of April 20th–21st (as the *facts* tell us).

And thus the "lesson" speaks *against* the wiseacres of the *Novaya Zhizhn*.

Secondly, if the Bolsheviks did not even aim at an insurrection on July 3rd–4th—if not a single branch of the Bolsheviks even raised this question— the reason of this is *outside* our dispute with the *Novaya Zhizhn*. For we are discussing the lessons of a civil war— that is, of an insurrection, and not of the circumstances when a revolutionary party, knowing that it has not a majority on its side, abstains from the idea of insurrection. As it is well known that the Bolsheviks received a majority in the Soviets both in the capital and in the country (more than 49 per cent. of votes in Moscow) *much later* than July 1917, therefore, once more the "lessons" to be drawn are again, once again, not at all those which the perfectly charming *Novaya Zhizhn* lady would like to draw. No, no; you had better not take to politics, citizens of the *Novaya Zhizhn* !

If a revolutionary party has no majority in the vanguard of the revolutionary classes and in the country, then there can be no question of insurrection. Besides this, insurrection requires (1) the cumulative growth of revolution on a general national scale; (2) the complete moral and political break-up of the old, for instance the "Coalition," government; (3) great vacillation amongst the intermediate elements—that is, among those who are not quite in favour of the government, although they fully supported it but yesterday. Why has the *Novaya Zhizhn*, in proceeding to discuss the lessons of July 3rd–5th, not even noticed this very important lesson? Because they are not politicians discussing political questions, but only members of a circle of intellectuals frightened out of their wits by the bourgeoisie. Further, and thirdly, the facts show that it is just *after* July 3rd–4th, precisely as a result of the revelation of the nature of the Messieurs Tseretellis' *July* policy, precisely because the *masses* have recognised the Bolsheviks to be *their* front-rank fighters and the "Socialist Coalitionists" to be traitors, that the *dissolution* of the Mensheviks and S.R.'s is now beginning. This break-up was already fully proved *even before* the Kornilov episode, by the elections of 20th August, in Petrograd, which gave a victory to the Bolsheviks and played havoc with the "Socialist block." The *Dielo Naroda*, not long ago, tried to disprove this, con-

cealing the totals regarding all parties,
but this is a self-deception and a decep-
tion of the reader. According to the
Dien of August 24th, referring only to
the towns, the percentage of votes for
the Cadets rose from 22 to 23 per cent.
and their absolute number of votes
decreased 40 per cent. The percentage
of votes for the Bolsheviks rose from
20 to 30 per cent. and their absolute
number of votes decreased only by 10
per cent.; the percentage of votes for
all the "intermediates" decreased from
58 to 44 per cent. and their absolute
number of votes decreased by 60 per
cent. (!!).

The dissolution of the S.R.'s and
Mensheviks, after the July days and up
to the Kornilov days, is also shown by
the growth of the "left" wing in each
party, reaching nearly 40 per cent.—the
"Nemesis" of the persecutions of the
Bolsheviks by the Kerenskys.

The proletarian party, in spite of its
"loss" of a few hundreds of its members,
has made gigantic strides as a result

Will the Bolsheviks

of July 3rd–4th, for precisely in these difficult days the *masses* came to comprehend and to recognise its devotion and the *traitorous* policy of the S.R.'s and Mensheviks. The "lesson," it appears, is quite, quite of a different nature from that taught by the *Novaya Zhizhn*. Leave not the seething masses for the "placid democracy," and, if you start insurrection, then take the offensive whilst the forces of the enemy are still scattered—seize the enemy unawares. Is that not so, gentlemen—you "also Marxists" of the *Novaya Zhizhn*? Or does "Marxism" consist in neglecting to take as the foundation for one's tactics an exact estimate of the *objective* position, and simply collecting in one heap, without rhyme or reason, without criticism, "civil war" and the "Soviet Congress and the summoning of the Constituent Assembly"?

But surely, gentlemen, this is simply ridiculous, it is nothing but a mockery of Marxism and of all logic in general.

If in the *objective* position of affairs

Maintain Power ?

there is no foundation for the sharpening of the class war to the point of "civil war," then why have you started talking about "civil war" when discussing the subject of the "Soviet Congress and the Constituent Assembly"? (This is exactly the title of the leader in the *Novaya Zhizhn*.)

In that case you should have told the reader clearly, and proved to him, that in the present objective position of affairs there is *no* foundation for civil war, and that, therefore, one can and must place at the head of one's tactics peaceful, constitutional, legal, judicial, and parliamentary "simple" things, such as the Soviet Congress and the Constituent Assembly; then one can hold the point of view that such a congress and such an assembly are really capable of *solving* things. If, however, there is the germ of the inevitability, or even probability, of civil war in the objective circumstances of the moment, if you have not talked of it merely at random, but clearly seeing, feeling, sensing that the circumstances are opportune for civil war, then how can you place at the apex of the angle the Soviet Congress or the Constituent Assembly? This is surely but mocking the hungry, tortured masses! What! Do you think the starving will agree to wait two months? Or that the devastation, regarding the growth of which you yourselves write daily, will consent to "wait" for the Soviet Congress or for the Constituent Assembly? Or will the German offensive, in the absence of serious steps towards peace (that is, in the absence of a formal proposition of a just peace to all the belligerents) on our side, agree to "wait" until the meeting of the Soviet Congress and the Constituent Assembly? Or have you facts that allow you to conclude that the history of the Russian revolution, which has been proceeding so extraordinarily stormily and with such rapid *tempo* from February 28th to September 30th, will assume between October 1st and November

Maintain Power?

29th an episcopally solemn, quiet, peaceful, legally balanced pace, excluding all explosions, leaps, defeats in the war, or economic crises? Or will the army at the front, of which the non-Bolshevik officer Dubasov declared officially in the name of the front that "it will not fight," will this army begin again to starve and freeze quietly until the date "fixed"? Or will the peasant risings cease to be an element of civil war, merely because you designate them as "anarchical," or as "pogromist," or because Kerensky sends military forces *against the peasants*? Or is quiet, regular, really honest work by the government for the summoning of the Constituent Assembly by November 29th possible, conceivable in a *peasant* country when at the same time the government is busy *suppressing* peasant risings there?

Do not laugh at the "confusion in the Smolny Institute," gentlemen! Your own confusion is no less. You reply to the stern question of civil

The Bolsheviks

war by means of confused phrases and pitiful constitutional illusions. This is why I say that if the Bolsheviks were to submit to such a frame of mind they would ruin both their party and their revolution.

N. LENIN.

October 1st, 1917.